COMIC CHARACTERS

CAVAN SCOTT

Badger Publishing Limited
Oldmedow Road,
Hardwick Industrial Estate,
King's Lynn PE30 4JJ
Telephone: 01438 791037

www.badgerlearning.co.uk

2 4 6 8 10 9 7 5 3 1

Comic Characters ISBN 978-1-78464-036-1

Publisher: Susan Ross
Senior Editor: Danny Pearson
Publishing Assistant: Claire Morgan
Designer: Fiona Grant
Series Consultant: Dee Reid

Photos: Cover Image: Mike Pont/Getty Images
Page 5: Hulton Archive/Getty Images
Page 6: © Heritage Image Partnership Ltd/Alamy
Page 8: Randy Mayor
Page 9: Courtesy Everett Collection/REX
Page 10: © DC Thomson & Co. Ltd.
Page 11: © DC Thomson & Co. Ltd.
Page 12: © DC Thomson & Co. Ltd.
Page 14: Hulton Archive/Getty Images
Page 15: © Art Directors & TRIP/Alamy
Page 16: Mike Hollist/Daily Mail /REX
Page 17: © Moviestore collection Ltd/Alamy
Page 18: © Tony Worpole/Alamy
Page 19: EC Comics
Page 20: EC Comics
Page 21: © JHPhoto/Alamy
Page 22: © FILM STILLS/Alamy
Page 23: Moviestore Collection/REX
Page 24: © Art Directors & TRIP/Alamy
Page 26: © Photos 12/Alamy
Page 27: © Moviestore collection Ltd/Alamy
Page 28: © Cultura Creative (RF)/Alamy
Page 29: © FILM STILLS/Alamy

Attempts to contact all copyright holders have been made.
If any omitted would care to contact Badger Learning, we will be happy to make appropriate arrangements.

Contents

Vocabulary

appearance	hilarious
disguised	mischievous
encouraged	naughtiest
generation	radioactive

1. COMICS OF LONG AGO

Comics are older than you think.

In 17th Century Britain, newspapers called broadsheets were handed out on street corners.

The most popular ones were those with gory drawings of people getting their heads chopped off or being hanged by the neck!

Soon, the broadsheets also started to print jokey pictures of famous people. These became the world's first cartoons.

One hundred and fifty years ago, lots of newspapers had cartoons.

They were like the cartoons we see today with speech bubbles and funny captions.

The first comic written just for children went on sale in England in 1914. It was called *The Rainbow* and it starred the mischievous Tiger Tim.

It was such a success that comics for children soon became more popular than comics for adults.

American newspapers had comic strips too.

In 1929, Popeye the Sailor Man first appeared in a daily comic strip.

Popeye got super-strength and bulging muscles every time he ate spinach. It encouraged children to eat more vegetables.

Popeye was so popular as a comic strip, it was made into a cartoon for television.

Popeye was an easy-going sailor but when something really annoyed him he would eat a can of spinach and sing:

I'm strong to the finish 'cos I eats me spinach. I'm Popeye the Sailor Man!

One of the most popular brands of spinach in America is called Popeye!

2. NAUGHTY BOYS AND GIRLS

In 1937, the first issue of the comic called *The Dandy* hit the British shops.

It was an instant success, with hilarious characters like Korky, a crazy cat who was always getting in trouble.

Desperate Dan was another character in *The Dandy*.

Dan was a super-strong cowboy. His favourite meal was cow pie, complete with horns and a tail!

A year later, *The Dandy* was joined by another comic – *The Beano*.

However, the most famous character in *The Beano* – Dennis the Menace – didn't appear until the 1950s.

Dennis the Menace is the world's wildest boy. He is easy to spot with his spikey hair and best friend Gnasher the dog!

WOW! facts

Dennis wears a red and black jumper because those colours were the cheapest inks to use when he first appeared!

By the 1980s, newsagents were full of weekly kids' comics with names like *Buster*, *Nutty* and *Whoopie*.

However, in the 1990s they started to be replaced by comics based on the latest toys and TV shows.

Today, *The Beano* is the only survivor from the early days of British comics.

Over the years, British comics have given away free gifts to attract new readers.

The first issue of the *The Dandy* came with a whistle, while the first issue of *The Beano* gave away a free mask.

Other popular gifts over the years included jumping frogs, potato guns and whoopee cushions.

Today, most comics come with a number of free gifts, from toys to stickers.

3. RISE OF THE SUPERHEROES

While children in Britain loved comics with funny characters, the first American comic books were all about adventure.

They were full of cops, gangsters or science fiction heroes.

Then, in 1938, a new kind of hero made an appearance. *Action Comics* introduced the world to Superman, an alien from the planet Krypton.

Superman had amazing powers:
- He could run faster than a speeding bullet.
- He could lift incredible weights.
- He could see through solid objects.

Superman had a secret identity. He disguised himself as journalist Clark Kent by putting on a pair of glasses!

WOW! facts

In the first comics Superman couldn't fly. He had to jump over tall buildings instead!

Batman

Unlike Superman, Batman had no special powers.

He relied on quick thinking and athletic skills to fight crime. Together with Robin, the Boy Wonder, he fought evil supervillains such as the Joker, the Penguin and Catwoman.

Both Superman and Batman were published by a company called DC Comics.

In 1942, DC Comics introduced a new female superhero.

Wonder Woman had some amazing super powers.

- She was as strong as Superman.
- She had magic bullet-proof bracelets.
- She even flew an invisible aeroplane!

DC Comics' superheroes were so popular that they soon started to appear in their own radio and TV shows.

4. HORROR COMICS

By the 1950s, comics were more popular than ever.

There was only one problem – they nearly got banned!

In America, comics were getting more and more violent.

War comics had always sold well, but now comic publishers were bringing out horror comics full of blood and gore.

Every month, readers would scare themselves silly reading horror comics like *Tales from the Crypt* and *The Haunt of Fear*.

They became so popular that adults started to worry what effect the creepy stories were having on children.

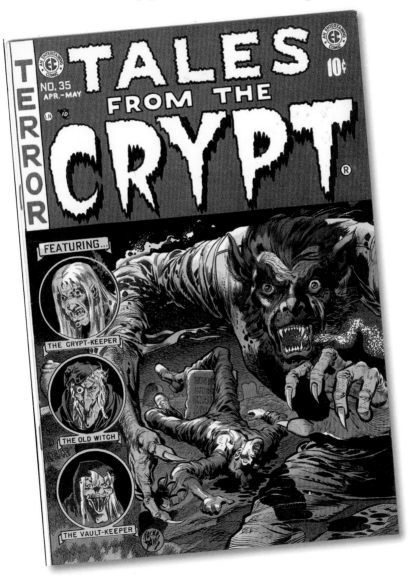

Newspapers called for comics to be banned.

In America, a list of rules was set up by the government.

The rules said that if a comic was too violent or scary it simply couldn't be sold!

The rules for comics:

- Not too violent.

- No vampires, werewolves or zombies.

- Criminals must always be caught.

The comic publishers decided that it was too difficult to publish horror stories under the new rules, so a company called Marvel Comics decided to introduce a new generation of superheroes instead.

5. THE MIGHTY WORLD OF MARVEL

The Fantastic Four appeared in 1961.

Each of the Fantastic Four had a superpower.

- Mr Fantastic could stretch his body like rubber.
- Invisible Girl could disappear.
- The Human Torch could control fire.
- The Thing, an orange rocky monster, was super-strong.

The Incredible Hulk

The Thing was the most popular character so in 1962 the comic writers created another monster – The Incredible Hulk.

Every time scientist Bruce Banner lost his temper he transformed into The Incredible Hulk.

The angrier he was, the more powerful he became.

In the very first Incredible Hulk comic, his skin was grey, not green!

Spider-Man

Marvel's most famous creation swung into action in 1962.

Peter Parker was an ordinary schoolboy who was bitten by a radioactive spider.

Suddenly, he had super strength and could climb walls like a spider.

He had become the Amazing Spider-Man.

Spider-Man and The Incredible Hulk both had their own successful TV series and later starred in some very successful films.

The next Marvel Comics super team was The Mighty Avengers!

The first Mighty Avengers were:
- Thor
- The Incredible Hulk
- Iron Man
- Wasp
- Ant-Man

6. BIG SCREEN SUPERHEROES

Today, computer graphics can help bring comic characters to life on the big screen like never before.

The Avengers movies tell the stories of a group of superheroes who protect planet Earth from attack.

They are led by Captain America, a super-soldier from World War Two.

The X-Men films are also based on Marvel comic characters.

Superheroes like Wolverine are born with special powers but they are not always trusted by the rest of the human race.

It's not just Marvel superheroes that have returned to the big screen.

Superman and Batman have also been updated for the 21st Century.

7. DIGITAL COMICS

There are now more comics than ever, and not just full of superheroes.

You can find romantic comics, spy comics, crime comics and war comics. There are even horror comics again.

Comics can be read in lots of different ways.

Many people now read comics on tablets and computers. New issues appear within seconds of being published.

Brand new comics can also be found on the internet. Some webcomics are short daily strips like newspaper cartoons, while others are longer stories broken up into weekly episodes.

The way we read comics may have changed, but our favourite comic characters keep coming back, time and time again.

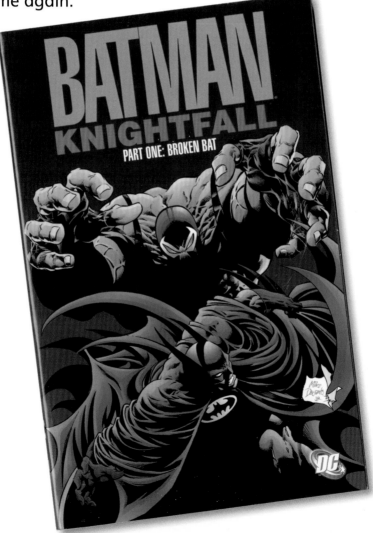

Comic character quiz

Fit the description to the character.

Description	Character
Eats spinach	Mr Fantastic
Can climb up walls	Superman
Flies an invisible aeroplane	Popeye
Eats cow pie	The Incredible Hulk
Can stretch his body like rubber	Spider-man
Has green skin	Desperate Dan
Can see through solid objects	Wonder Woman

Questions

When did the first comic for children go on sale in England? *(page 7)*

What food did Popeye eat to make him stronger? *(page 8)*

When did Superman first appear and what was the name of the comic series? *(page 14)*

Name three villains Batman has fought against. *(page 16)*

What was the name of the scientist who turned into The Incredible Hulk every time he lost his temper? *(page 23)*

Name four of the first Mighty Avengers. *(page 25)*

INDEX